STEM *trailblazer*

YOUTUBE FOUNDERS

STEVE CHEN, CHAD HURLEY, AND JAWED KARIM

PATRICIA WOOSTER

Lerner Publications Company
Minneapolis

Lerner Publications Company
A division of Lerner Publishing Group, Inc.
241 First Avenue North
Minneapolis, MN 55401 U.S.A.

For reading levels and more information, look up this title at www.lernerbooks.com.

Content Consultant: Patricia G. Lange, Ph.D., Assistant Professor, Critical Studies, California College of the Arts

Library of Congress Cataloging-in-Publication Data

Wooster, Patricia.
  YouTube founders Steve Chen, Chad Hurley, and Jawed Karim / by Patricia Wooster.
    p.   cm. — (STEM trailblazer bios)
  Includes index.
  ISBN 978-1-4677-2457-9 (lib. bdg. : alk. paper)
  ISBN 978-1-4677-2482-1 (eBook)
  1. Hurley, Chad, 1977– 2. Chen, Steve, 1978– 3. Karim, Jawed, 1979–
4. Telecommunications engineers—United States—Biography—Juvenile literature.
5. Webmasters—United States—Biography—Juvenile literature. 6. Computer programmers—United States—Biography—Juvenile literature. 7. Businesspeople—United States—Biography—Juvenile literature. 8. YouTube (Electronic resource)—Juvenile literature. 9. YouTube (Firm)—Juvenile literature. 10. Internet videos—Juvenile literature. 11. Online social networks—Juvenile literature. I. Title.
  TK5102.54.W66 2014
  384.3'3—dc23 [B]   2013026971

Manufactured in the United States of America
1 – PC – 12/31/13

The images in this book are used with the permission of: © Jakub Krechowicz/Shutterstock Images, p. 4; © Martin Kilmek/Zuma Press/Newscom, p. 5; © Lionel Cironneau/AP Images, p. 6; © loops7/iStockphoto, p. 7; © Mark Lennihan/AP Images, p. 8; © Henryk Sadura/Shutterstock Images, p. 9; © The News-Gazette, Darrell Hoemann/AP Images, p. 10; © Shutterstock Images, p. 11; © Eric Risberg/AP Images, p. 12; © Yakov Lapitsky, p. 14; © iStockphoto, pp. 15, 25; © Stock Connection/SuperStock, p. 16; © Philippe Wojazer/Corbis, p. 17; © Tony Avelar/AP Images, p. 18; © Eric Vega/iStockphoto, p. 19; © Noah Berger/AP Images, p. 21; © Stephen Chernin/AP Images, p. 22; © Jochen Tack/SuperStock, p. 26; © Jawed/Wikimedia Commons, p. 27.

Front cover: © Zuma/Martin Klimek/Newscom

Main body text set in Adrianna Regular 13/22. Typeface provided by Chank.

CONTENTS

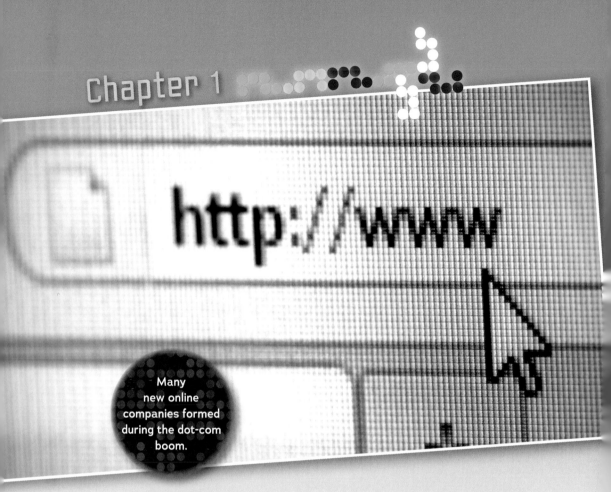

Chapter 1

Many new online companies formed during the dot-com boom.

INTERNET EXPLOSION
BRINGS FRIENDS TOGETHER

In the late 1990s, new Internet companies were starting every day. Everyone was talking about these new dot-com businesses. Most of the people starting them were young adults with fresh ideas.

Chad Hurley, Steve Chen, and Jawed Karim met while working together at a new company in the dot-com boom. They had a fresh idea of their own. They wanted to create a website where people could share videos. They named their new website YouTube.

From top to bottom: Hurley, Chen, and Karim became friends while working together.

Even from an early age, Hurley was interested in computers.

CHAD HURLEY

Chad Hurley was born on July 21, 1977. He grew up in Birdsboro, Pennsylvania. Hurley was interested in drawing. As a child, he sold artwork on his front lawn. In ninth grade, he won an electronics competition for building an **amplifier**.

Hurley's love of art led him to computers and **graphic design**. He spent hours playing online games and studying web design. He earned a fine arts degree from Indiana University of Pennsylvania. In 1999, he became the first graphic designer at PayPal. PayPal was a huge part of the Internet boom. It let people pay for things over the Internet with credit cards and bank transfers. Hurley got the job when he created PayPal's logo, or symbol, during his job interview.

Hurley designed PayPal's company logo. PayPal started using this updated logo in 2007.

STEVE CHEN

Steve Chen was born in Taiwan on August 18, 1978. His family moved to the United States when he was eight years old. He went to high school at the Illinois Mathematics and Science Academy (IMSA). At IMSA, students did college-level work. Chen enjoyed studying engineering. He also spent a lot of time on the Internet.

TECH TALK

From 1997 to 2000, people were racing to the Internet with new technology and new companies. Time spent developing new ideas was paying off in big ways. When asked about this time period, Chen said, "There's a fervor, a willingness to take a risk—to throw two or three months into something to see if it works."

After high school, Chen studied computer science at the University of Illinois. In 1999, he went to work at PayPal. Chen wrote software programs for the company and was good at solving computer problems. He met Chad Hurley there.

Chen attended the University of Illinois at Urbana-Champaign in Champaign, Illinois.

Karim talks with the chancellor at the University of Illinois graduation ceremony.

JAWED KARIM

Jawed Karim was born in Merseburg, Germany, on October 28, 1979. His family moved to the United States when he was thirteen. His parents are both high-tech researchers. In high school, Karim wrote computer programs. He posted them on the Internet for free. He helped set up his school's e-mail system.

Karim also went to the University of Illinois to study computer science. He got work experience through several

internships at technology companies. In 2000, Karim went to work for PayPal. He helped the company design their online antifraud, or security, system.

COWORKERS AND FRIENDS

Chen, Hurley, and Karim became friends at PayPal. They often met outside of work at a café. They brainstormed ideas to start their own company. The Internet was growing quickly. They wanted to create technology that would let people use the Internet in new ways.

Karim's family moved to Minnesota, where his mother became a biochemistry research professor at the University of Minnesota.

Chapter 2

A video that Chen and Hurley filmed of their friends sparked the idea for YouTube.

YOUTUBE:
A NEW WEBSITE

In January 2005, Chen had a dinner party at his house with some friends. Chen and Hurley used a **camcorder** to record video and sound of the party. Afterward, they wanted to share the videos with their friends. The video files were too big to send by e-mail. Photo-sharing websites such as Flickr and Shutterfly were becoming popular. But the friends couldn't find any websites for sharing their own videos. They brainstormed with Karim, and the three decided to create a website to share videos. They wanted anybody to be able to use it.

On February 15, 2005, Hurley, Chen, and Karim started building their new website. The name YouTube was a play on calling TV "the tube." This was a chance for Hurley, Chen, and Karim to add something new to the Internet.

GOALS FOR YOUTUBE

Hurley, Chen, and Karim made a list of goals for their new company. These goals would help set YouTube apart from other companies on the Internet. Their main goal was to make YouTube easy to use. Website users would be able to post and watch videos without having to buy or use extra software. The founders also wanted the videos to be organized. Then people new to the Internet or without a lot of Internet experience could use YouTube.

0:05 / 0:20

Karim's video about an elephant's trunk has been watched more than eleven million times!

YOUTUBE'S FIRST VIDEO

On April 23, 2005, Karim posted the first video on YouTube. It was filmed at the San Diego Zoo in California, in front of the elephants. "Me at the Zoo" is only eighteen seconds long. Karim created the video to test how the website worked.

CHOOSING JOBS

The founders decided to split up the work based on their skills. Hurley used his art skills to design the look of the website. He created the YouTube logo. He also started tagging and labeling videos as people added them. This made the videos easier for people to find.

Hurley designed YouTube's famous logo.

Chen was in charge of making sure the website worked. He made sure the videos played right away and with no problems. Karim used his computer programming skills to help get YouTube running. He worked with Hurley and Chen to make sure the website looked great and ran smoothly.

GATHERING USERS

Hurley used his creative skills to get more people to the site. He started a contest that gave away Apple iPods. One was given away to a different YouTube user every day for two months. People earned points for signing up friends or posting videos. Every point gave a person a better chance at winning the iPod.

Hurley's contest gave away free iPod Nanos to new YouTube users, attracting more people to the website.

Hurley and Chen pose for pictures together after a news conference in Paris in 2007.

When more visitors came to post and watch videos, the website slowed down. Videos were being added to the site so quickly it was running out of storage. It needed more bandwidth to keep the website running quickly. But this cost money. In November 2005, YouTube got a loan for $3.5 million. Chen and Karim were able to hire more than sixty people to help them with the website.

YOUTUBE GROWS

Just one year after YouTube started, more than 100 million videos were on the site. Posting videos on the site was so easy. Anyone with a video camera and an Internet connection could share a video with people in different parts of the world.

Hurley and Chen pose for a fun picture in their California office in 2006.

Some home videos, such as "Charlie Bit My Finger," have become hits on YouTube.

YouTube started out as a video-sharing website with many personal home videos. "How-to" videos started popping up where people could learn how to do anything from changing the oil in a car to doing a handstand. Chen, Hurley, and Karim discovered that many people liked sharing videos. And even more people enjoyed watching them.

Hurley became president of the company. He was creative and enjoyed coming up with new ideas. Chen became the chief technology officer. He kept improving the way the site worked. Karim chose a different path. He wanted to go back to college. He worked as a consultant, or person who gives advice, for the company.

Hurley and Chen spent most of their time just keeping the website working. On October 9, 2006, Google bought YouTube for $1.65 billion. Hurley and Chen were excited to work with such a large company. Now they could spend time adding new technology to the website. They had a lot of ideas for YouTube!

TECH TALK

Karim is often asked where his business ideas come from. "It's very simple," he explains. "I basically create things that I need myself. It just so happens that sometimes other people want to use it also."

Chen and Hurley were thrilled to work with Google when the tech giant bought their company in 2006.

Chapter 3

In 2007, Chen and Hurley received a Webby Award for their work on YouTube.

IMPROVING YOUTUBE

With Google running the business, Hurley and Chen had more time to spend on new ideas. They wanted people to stay on their website longer. Every day more and more videos were added. People were asking for more **features.** They wanted better video quality. And they wanted to access YouTube from any **device**. Hurley and Chen had a lot of work to do!

HERE, THERE, AND EVERYWHERE

Hurley and Chen wanted to launch YouTube in different countries. Hurley wanted people from around the world to share videos with one another. It was a great way to see what other people were doing in other parts of the world. Chen wanted to create new technology for each country's needs. With Google's help, Hurley and Chen started with nine countries, including Brazil, France, and the United Kingdom.

The founders also wanted to improve video quality. They knew people connected to the Internet at different speeds. So they wanted to make sure video clips looked good on any computer. They also wanted people to be able to use YouTube anywhere. YouTube and Google engineers worked together. They figured out how to send different video streams based on Internet speed. This let people with faster speeds get better video.

BETTER ALL THE TIME

The video quality and features on YouTube have just kept getting better! In 2009, Chen and Hurley made it possible for people to upload and watch 3D videos on the website. By 2011, someone could search YouTube videos from their Google account. And in 2013, YouTube began offering paid subscriptions. For a monthly fee, viewers could watch longer videos and even movies.

By the end of 2007, people could watch YouTube videos almost anywhere. YouTube's mobile app let people watch videos on their cell phones. People could also add videos to their own websites and blogs, or online personal journals. YouTube was everywhere!

Chapter 4

YouTube is
visited more than
three billion times
every day.

THE NEXT
BIG THING

YouTube is available in fifty-six countries and in sixty-one languages. Every minute, another 100 hours of video is loaded onto the site. In 2012, "Gangnam Style" by PSY became the most viewed video of all time.

WHERE ARE THEY NOW?

Karim always had an interest in school. He is working on another computer science degree at Stanford University. He may one day be a professor. In 2009, he helped start a company called Youniversity Ventures. He helps college students launch their business ideas. Karim loves to teach.

Karim continues to work on new technology for the Internet.

In 2010, Chen quit working for YouTube and Google. Hurley also left that year. They were ready to start new projects. They liked working together. They started a new company in 2011 called Avos Systems. They continue to create new ways for people to use the Internet.

Karim, Chen, and Hurley are all still very involved in technology. They want to change how people use the Internet. Every day they look for new challenges and ways to solve them. Who knows where their next great ideas will lead?

TECH TALK

The Internet lets people reach out to every corner of the world. "We hear stories of people using our services in places such as Africa, where children go to computer centers to view videos on YouTube and then say it's acting like a window to the world for them," Hurley said.

TIMELINE

1977

Chad Hurley is born on July 21 in Birdsboro, Pennsylvania.

1978

Steve Chen is born on August 18 in Taiwan.

1979

Jawed Karim is born on October 28 in Merseburg, Germany.

2000

Hurley, Chen, and Karim meet while working at PayPal.

2005

Hurley, Chen, and Karim register the name "YouTube" on February 15. On April 23, Karim posts YouTube's first video.

2006

Hurley, Chen, and Karim sell YouTube to Google on October 9.

2008

YouTube wins a Peabody Award for giving people a new way to express their freedom of speech.

2009

Karim starts Youniversity Ventures to help college students start businesses.

2011

Chen and Hurley start a company called Avos Systems to create new technology.

2012

"Gangnam Style" by PSY becomes the most viewed YouTube video of all time.

GLOSSARY

amplifier
an electronic device that increases power and sound

camcorder
a video and sound recorder

device
a piece of equipment, such as a computer, a phone, or a tablet computer

features
unique parts of something

graphic design
the skill of creating materials with text and pictures

internships
programs in which people can get job experience

SOURCE NOTES

9   Matt Marshall, "VCs Backing 'Magic' of Youth," *Silicon Valley*, February 12, 2006, http://www.siliconvalley.com/ci_5186421.

20 Carlyo, "Role Models in Science and Engineering: Jawed Karim – Computer Science Innovator," *USA Science and Engineering*, December 27, 2012, http://scienceblogs.com/usasciencefestival /2012/12/27/role-models-in-science-engineering-jawed-karim-computer-science-innovator/.

23 "YouTube's Chad Hurley: 'Surround Yourself with Great People,'" *Silicon Republic*, October, 29, 2010, http://www.siliconrepublic.com/start-ups /item/18556-youtubes-chad-hurley-sur.

27 Oliver Lindberg, "Chad Hurley and Steve Chen," *Net Magazine*, November 5, 2007, http://www.netmagazine.com/interviews /chad-hurley-and-steve-chen.

FURTHER INFORMATION

BOOKS

Duffield, Katy S. *Chad Hurley, Steve Chen, Jawed Karim: YouTube Creators.* Detroit: KidHaven, 2009. Read more about the founders of YouTube.

Kops, Deborah. *Were Early Computers Really the Size of a School Bus?: And Other Questions about Inventions.* Minneapolis: Lerner Publications, 2011. Find the answers to some fun questions about scientific inventions.

Parker, Steve. *Electronics and Technology.* New York: Parragon, 2010. Explore the technology behind many popular gadgets.

WEBSITES

BrainPOP
http://www.brainpop.com

Learn more about science and engineering.

Popular Science
http://www.popsci.com

Read about the latest developments in science and technology.

YouTube
http://www.youtube.com

Visit YouTube's official website.

INDEX

ABOUT THE AUTHOR

Patricia Wooster graduated from the University of Kansas with a degree in creative writing. She has written several nonfiction children's books. She lives in Tampa, Florida, with her husband, Scot, and two boys, Max and Jack.